★ SIMPLE MACHINES ★

pulleys

VALERIE BODDEN

Published by Creative Education
P.O. Box 227, Mankato, Minnesota 56002
Creative Education is an imprint of The Creative Company
www.thecreativecompany.us

Design and production by Liddy Walseth
Art direction by Rita Marshall
Printed by Corporate Graphics in the United States of America

Photographs by Dreamstime (Aperature8, O'jay Barbee, Sean Gladwell, Manuela
Klopsch, Xavier Marchant, VJ Matthew, Maxim Petrichuk), Getty Images (Navid
Baraty, Thomas Holton, Tony Howell, Hulton Collection, Dave King, Bert Kopperl/
Mansell/Time & Life Pictures, Alison Langley, Sandro Miller, Tom Paiva, George
Shepherd, SuperStock, Travel Ink), iStockphoto (Sabrina Dei Nobili)

Library of Congress Cataloging-in-Publication Data
Bodden, Valerie.
Pulleys / by Valerie Bodden.
p. cm. — (Simple machines)
Summary: A foundational look at pulleys, explaining how these simple machines
work and describing some common examples, such as gears and chains, that have
been used throughout history.
Includes index.
ISBN 978-1-60818-010-3
1. Pulleys—Juvenile literature. I. Title. II. Series.
TJ1103.B64 2011
621.8—dc22   2009048859
CPSIA: 040110 PO1140

First Edition
2 4 6 8 9 7 5 3 1

CREATIVE C EDUCATION

SIMPLE MACHINES

pulleys

VALERIE BODDEN

contents

Have you ever opened the blinds on a window or ridden a bike? You might not have known it, but you were using a pulley (*PULL-ee*). A pulley makes it easier to lift or move objects.

A pulley is a kind of simple machine. Simple machines have only a few moving parts. Some have no moving parts at all. Simple machines help people do WORK.

Pulleys help lift heavy containers onto ships

Pulleys are made up of two parts. One part is a wheel. The other part is a rope or chain. The wheel has a GROOVE in it. The rope or chain fits into the groove.

Ropes on
big pulleys
are thick
and strong

Fishermen use pulleys to lift nets full of fish

Pulleys are often used to lift heavy objects. The pulley wheel may be hung up high. A rope passes over it. The object is tied to one end of the rope. A person pulls down on the other end of the rope. As the person pulls the rope, the wheel turns, and the object is lifted up.

When you use a pulley, your body weight helps you pull down on the rope. This makes lifting something up with a pulley easier than lifting it without one.

Sometimes, people use ropes to CONNECT two or more pulleys. This makes lifting an object even easier. But it also means that the rope has to be pulled over a longer distance.

Pulleys
are used
on tall
ships and
deep wells

People have been using pulleys for thousands of years. Early pulleys were used to lift buckets of water from wells. Other pulleys were used to raise the sails on ships.

People still use pulleys today. Pulleys help lift flags to the tops of flagpoles. They pull CHAIR LIFTS up ski hills. The GEARS and chain on your bike are pulleys, too! They help turn the wheels.

People can ride up tall hills in chair lifts

Cranes have pulleys to help them lift heavy loads. Elevators use pulleys to move up and down. Pulleys are everywhere. Without them, we would have a much harder time lifting and moving the objects around us!

A CLOSER LOOK at *Pulleys*

THE GEARS AND CHAIN ON YOUR BIKE ARE A KIND OF PULLEY. BECAUSE OF THEM, YOU HAVE TO PUSH THE PEDALS AROUND ONLY ONCE TO MAKE YOUR WHEELS TURN MORE THAN ONE TIME. TRY IT AND SEE! MAKE A CHALK MARK ON THE TOP OF YOUR BIKE'S BACK WHEEL. RIDE YOUR BIKE FORWARD UNTIL YOUR PEDALS HAVE GONE AROUND ONE TIME. HAVE A FRIEND COUNT HOW MANY TIMES THE CHALK MARK GOES AROUND.

Glossary

chair lifts—seats that hang from a cable, or heavy rope, and carry people up and down hills

connect—join together

gears—wheels with teeth on the edges

groove—a narrow slit or path cut into something

work—using force (a push or pull) to move an object

Read More

Oxlade, Chris. *Pulleys.* Chicago: Heinemann Library, 2003.

Thales, Sharon. *Pulleys to the Rescue.* Mankato, Minn.: Capstone Press, 2007.

Web Sites

MIKIDS.com
http://www.mikids.com/Smachines.htm
Learn about the six kinds of simple machines and see examples of each one.

Simple Machines
http://staff.harrisonburg.k12.va.us/~mwampole/1-resources/simple-machines/index.html
Try to figure out which common objects are simple machines.

Index